MEN COLOURING BOOK
COLORING BOOK GIFT FOR MEN, DADS, FATHERS, HUSBANDS AND SPECIAL MEN EVERYWHERE

BELLA MOSLEY

Copyright © 2015 Bella Mosley
Men Colouring Book
All rights reserved.

Email: bella@colorartwork.com

Patterns may be used for your personal coloring pleasure. These patterns may not otherwise be reproduced for resale, or commercial use in whole or in part, in any form by any means without permission from the artist/ publisher.

ISBN-13: 978-1519142542

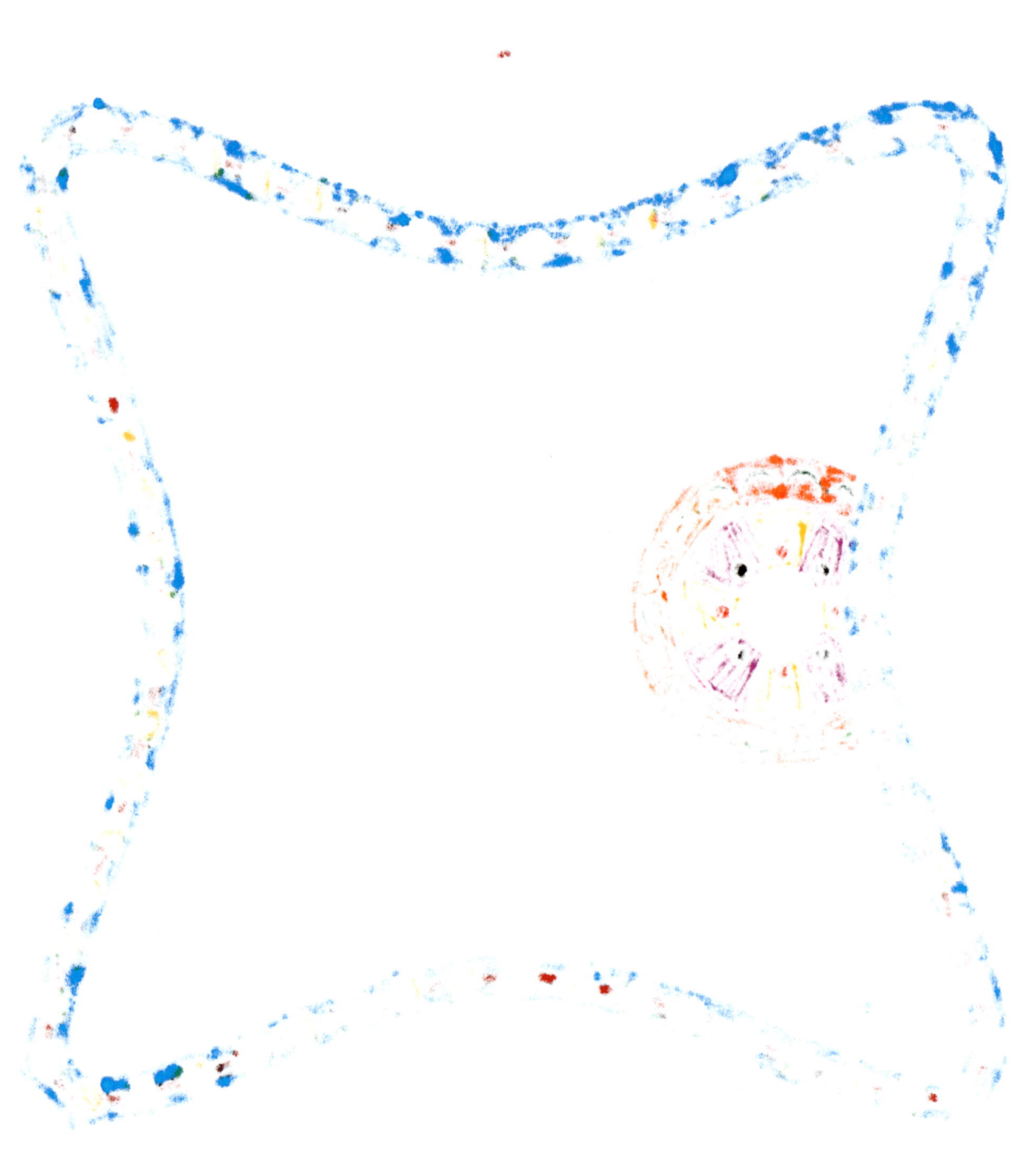

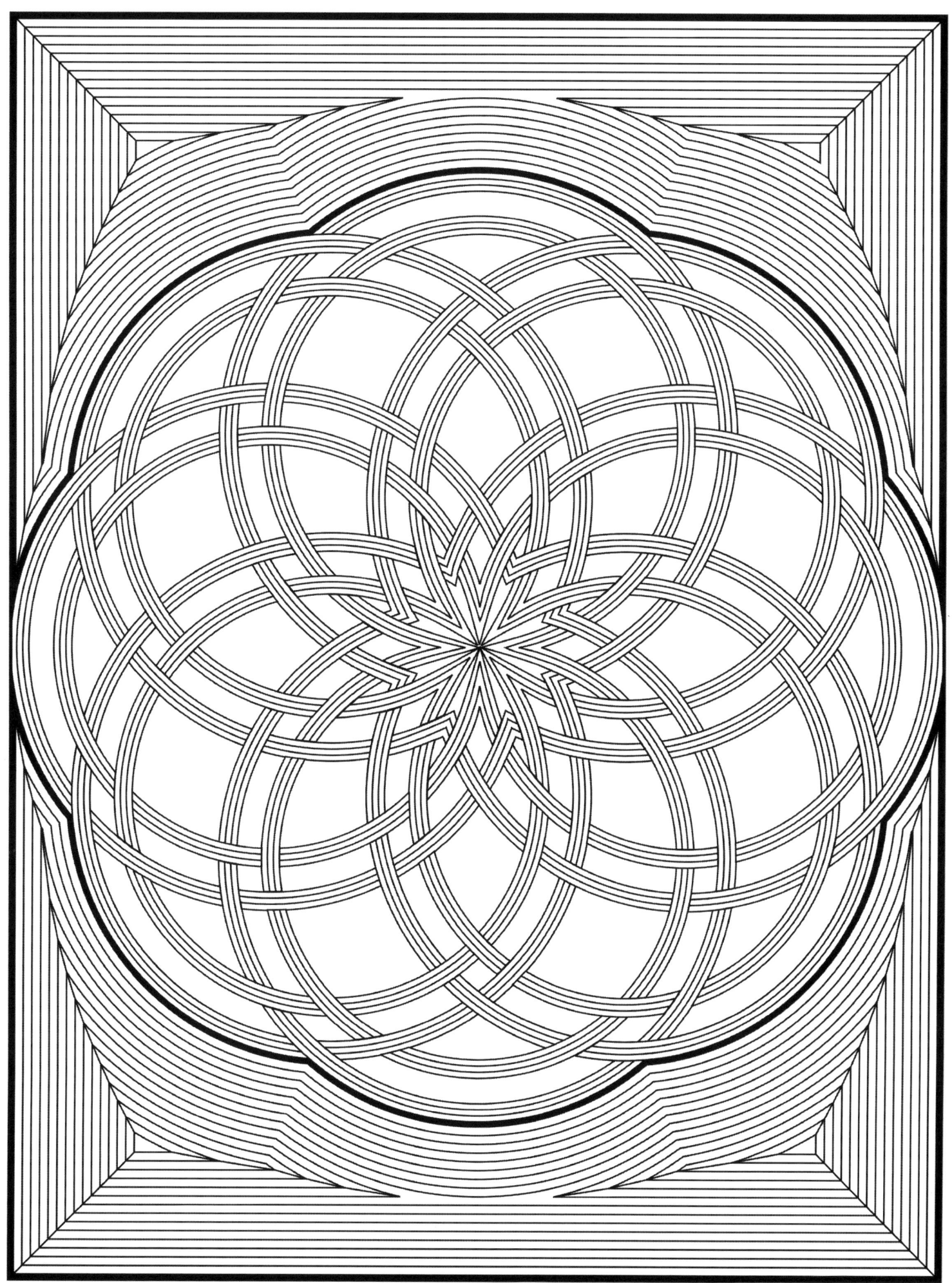

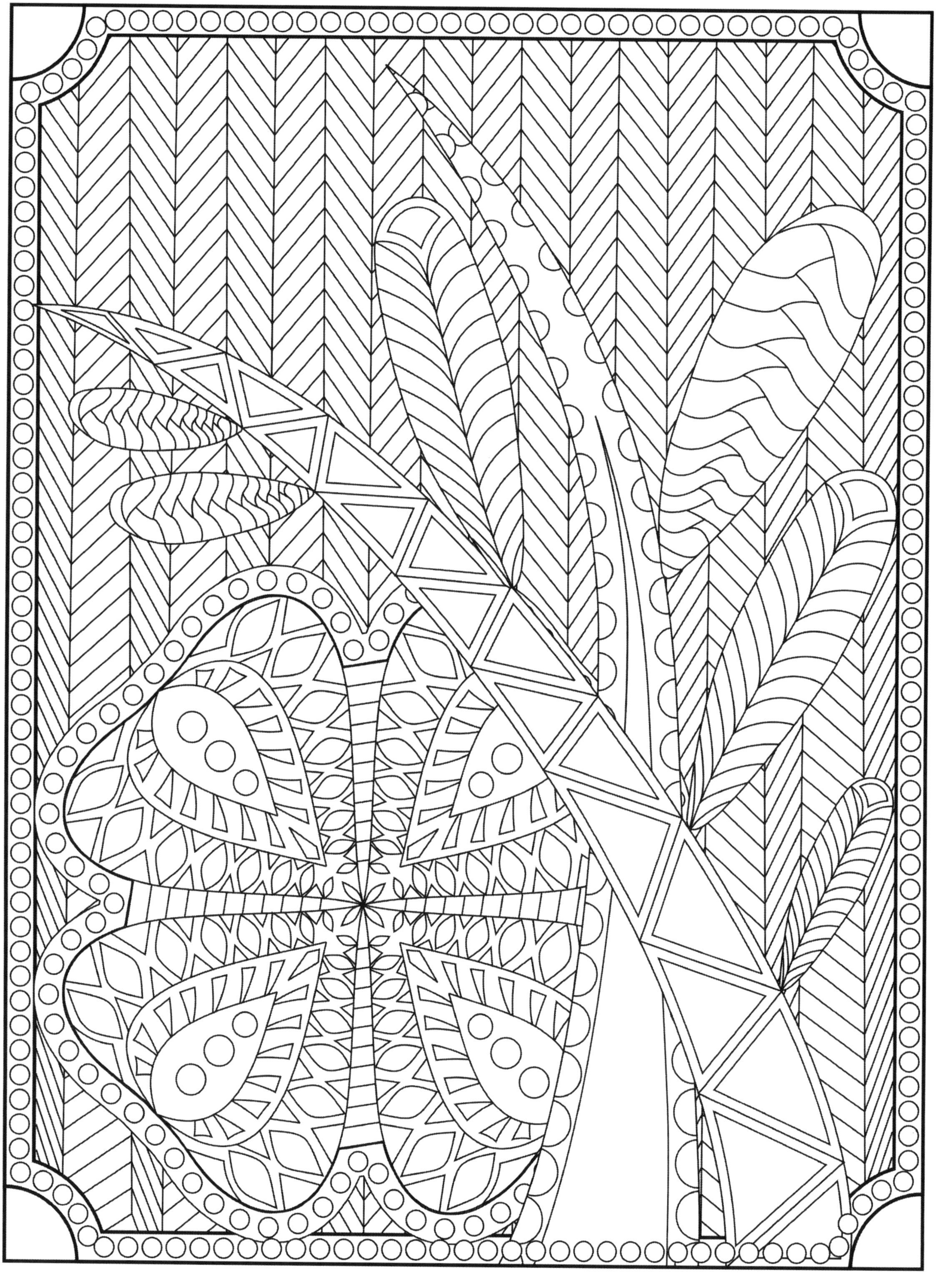

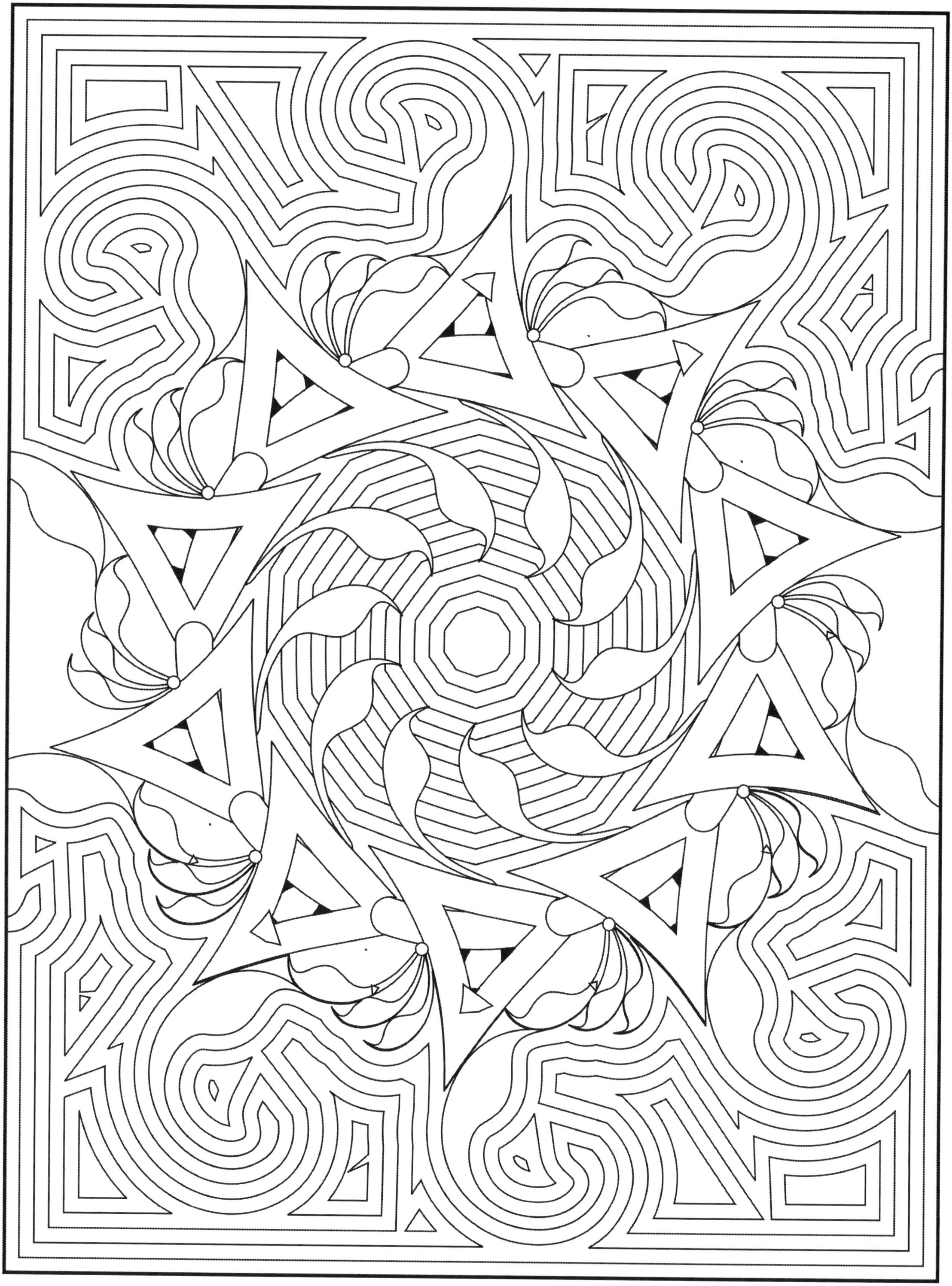

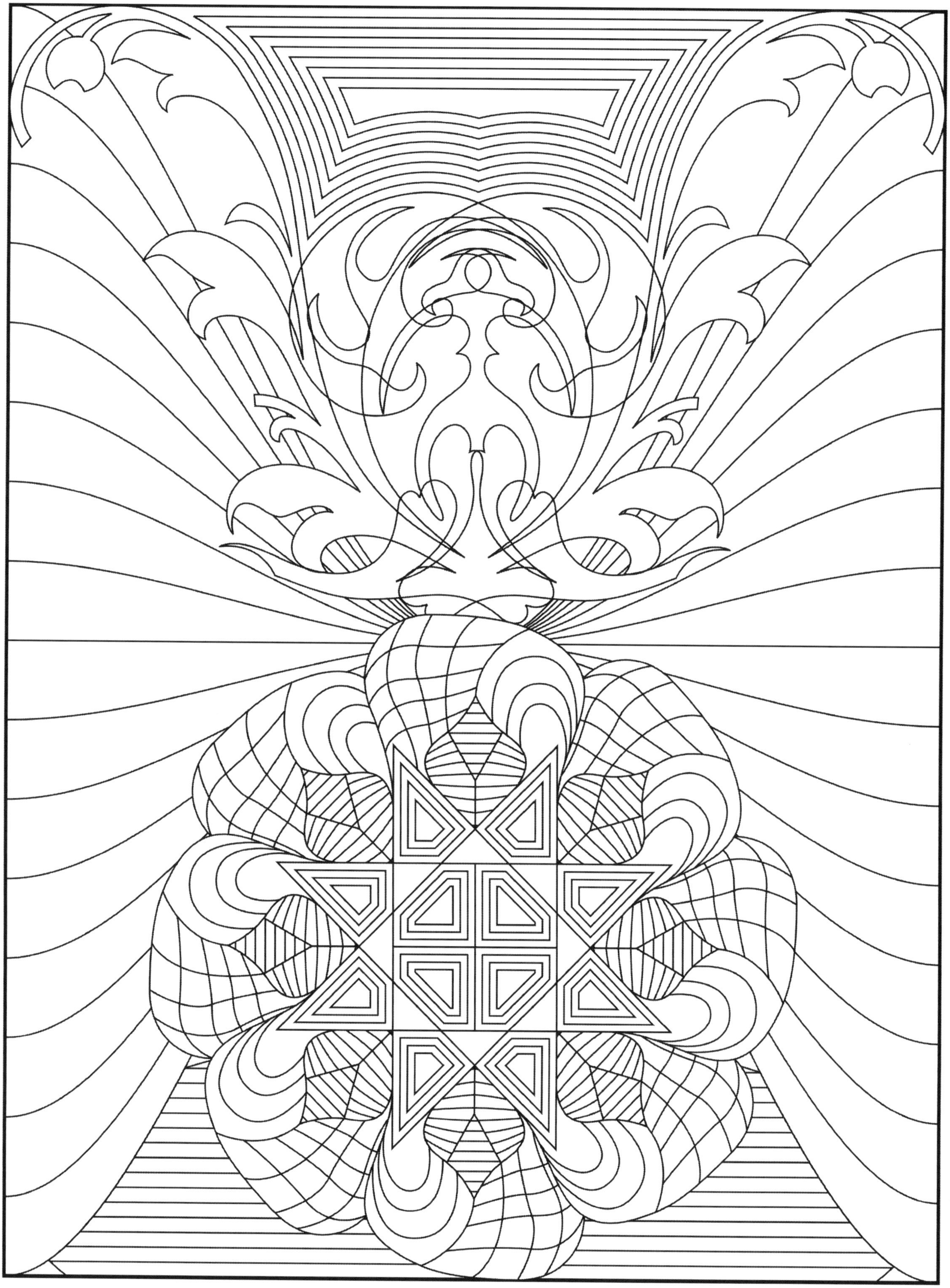

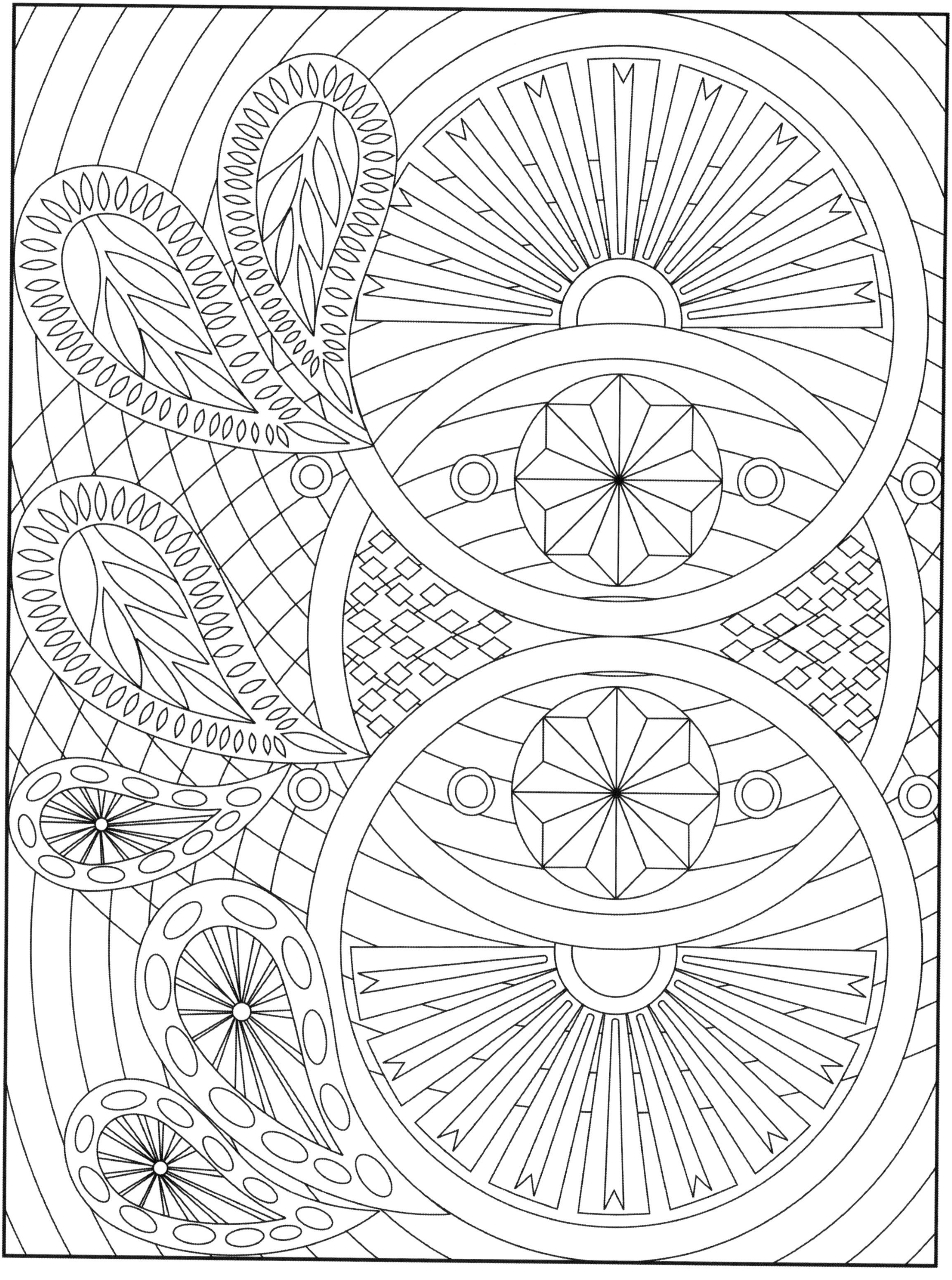

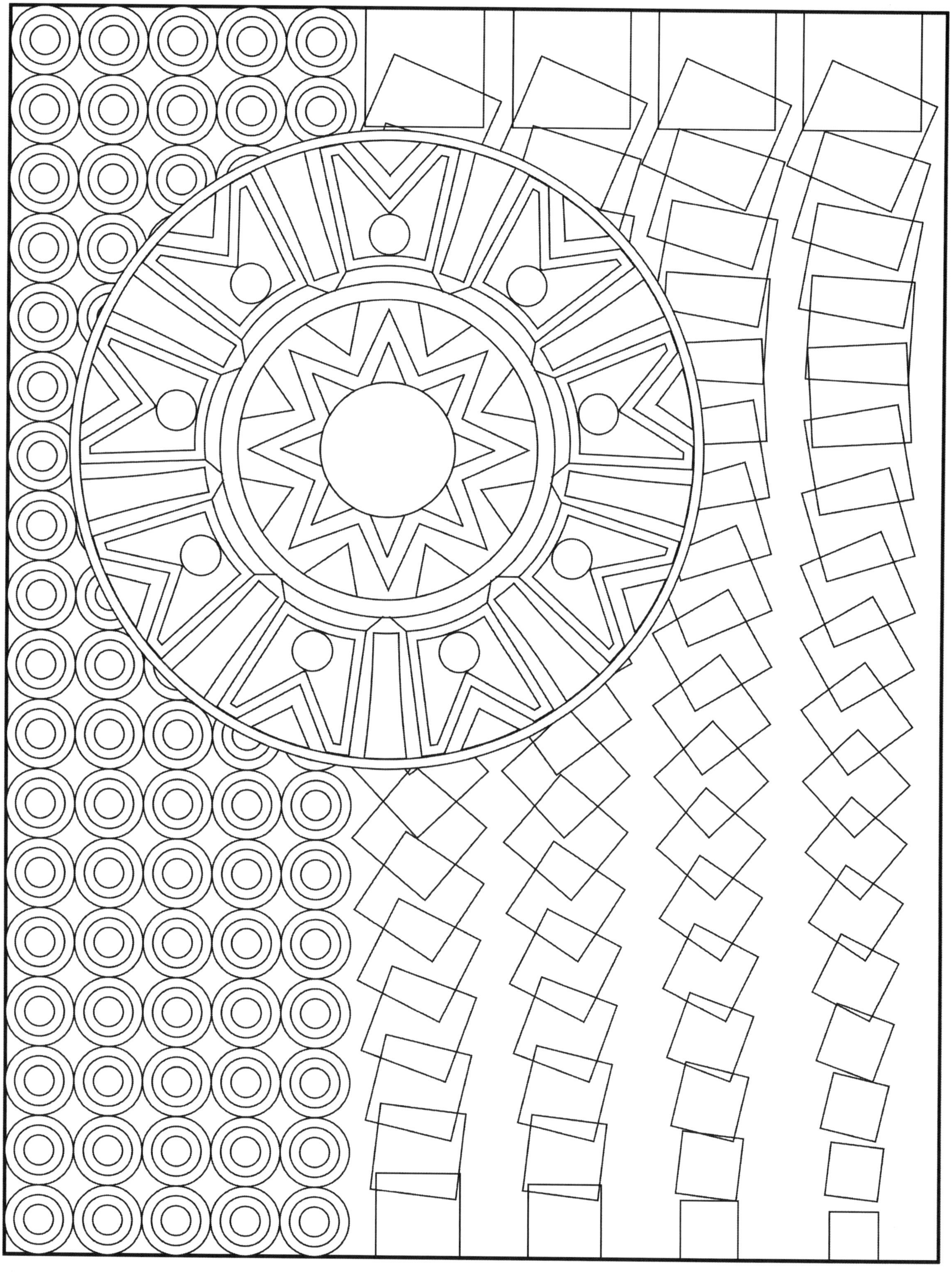

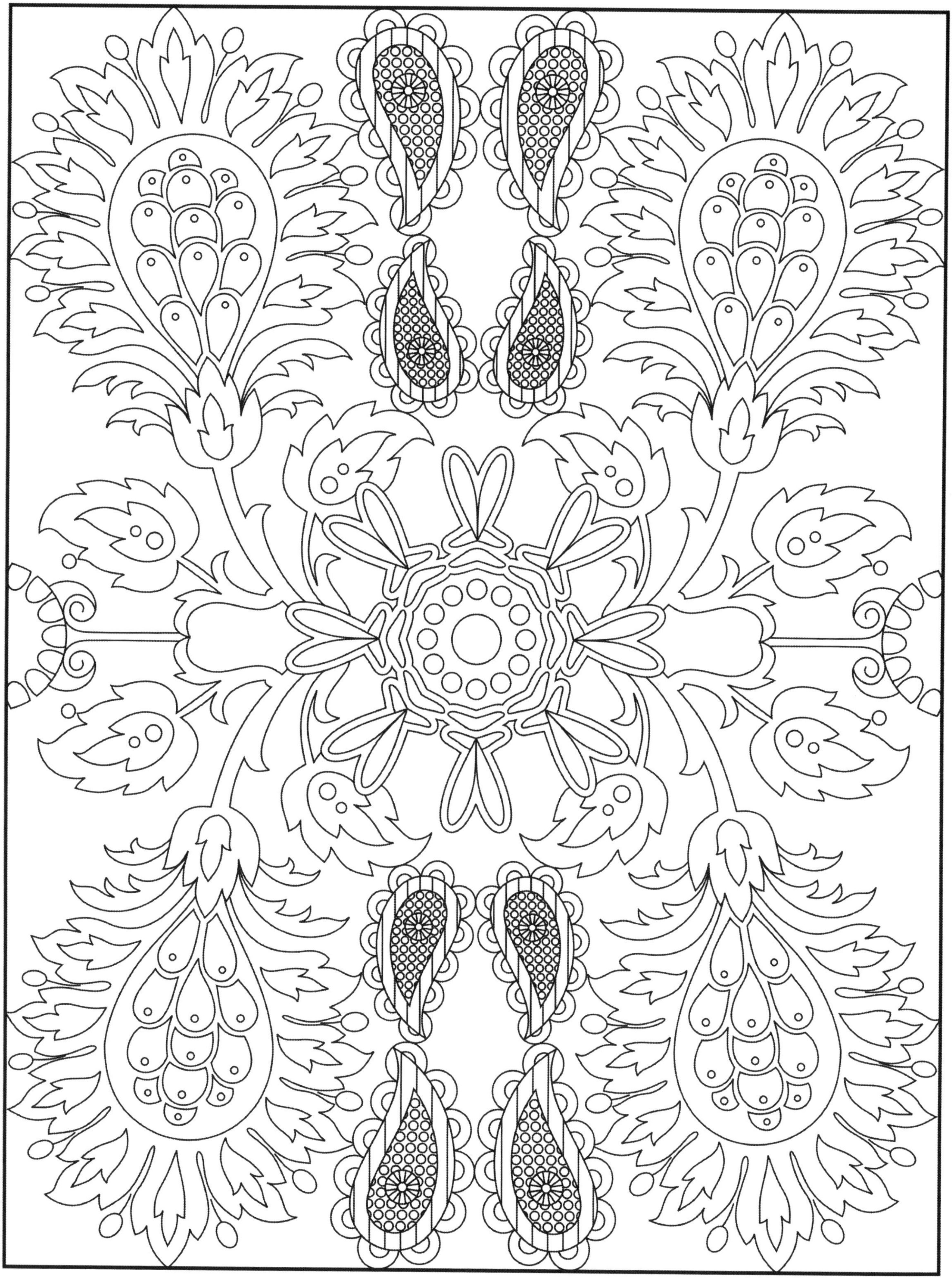

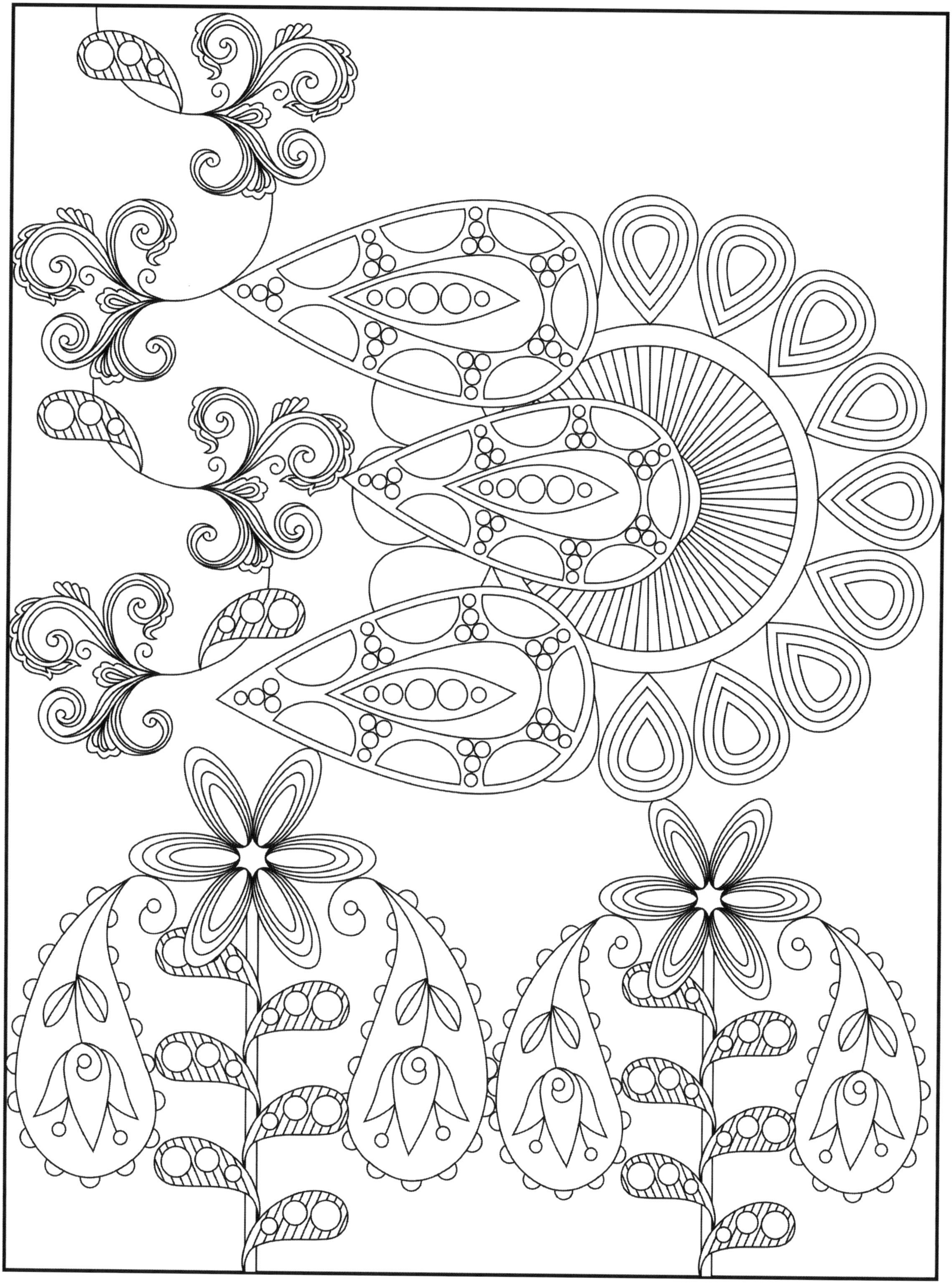

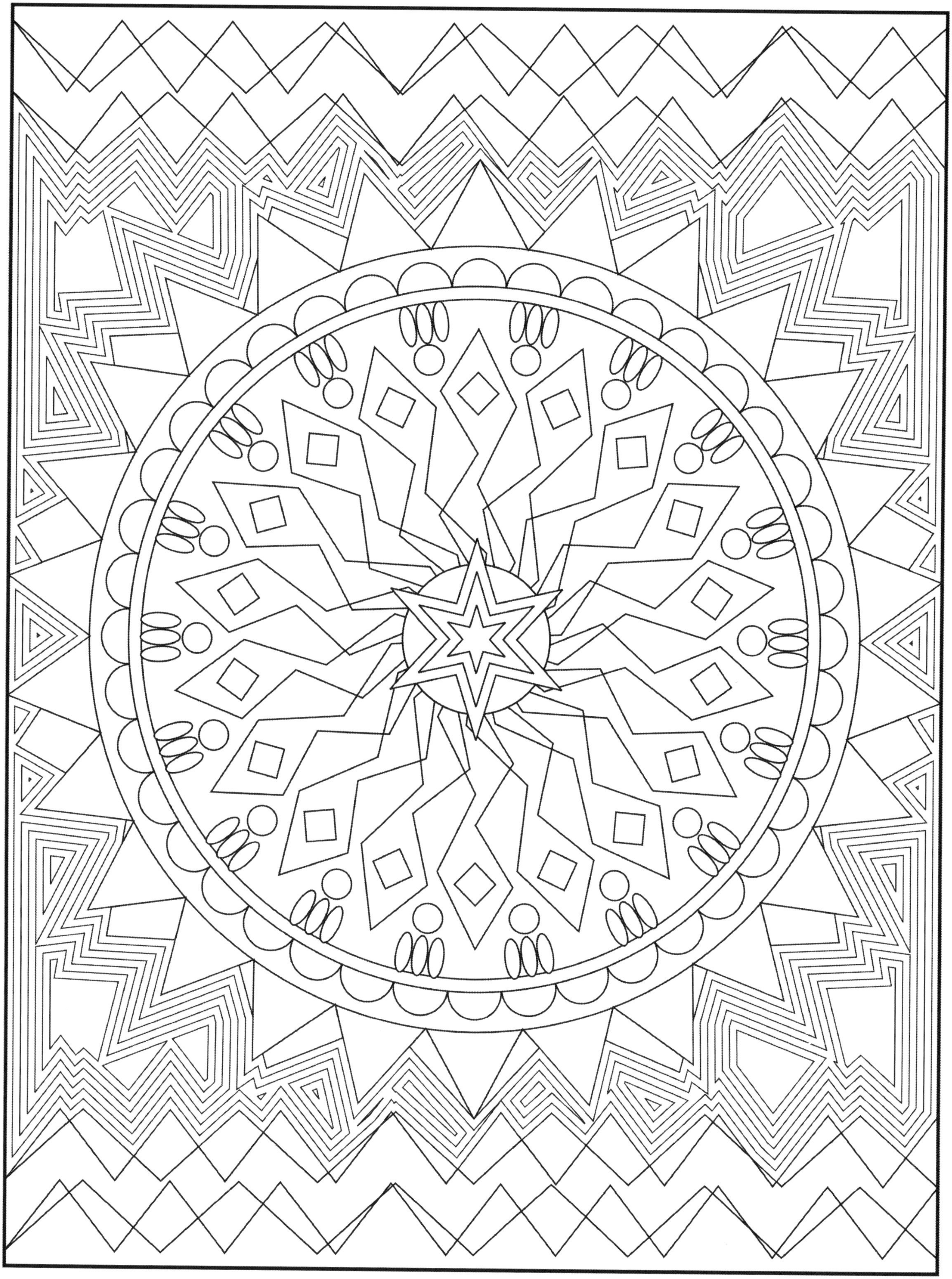

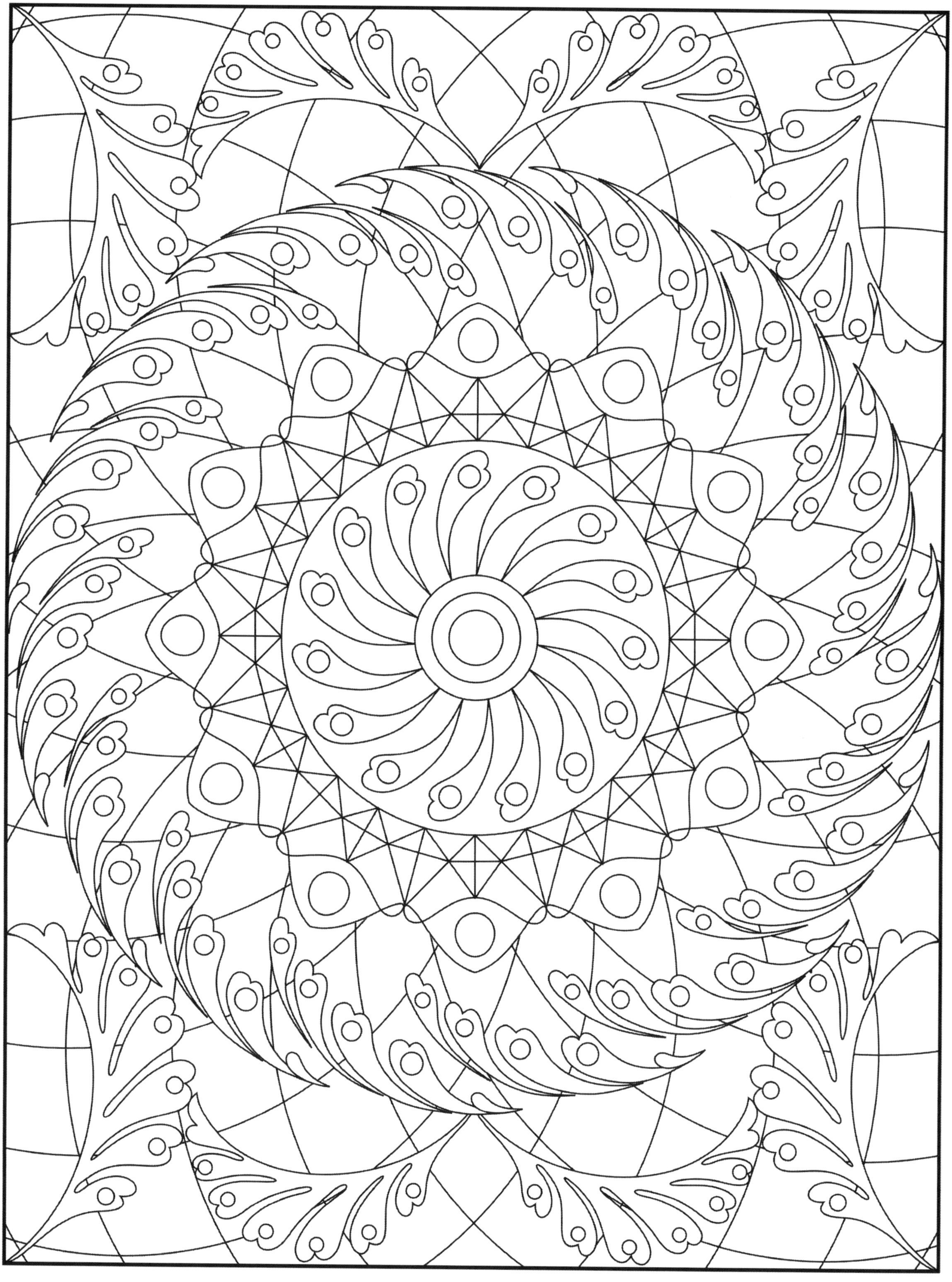

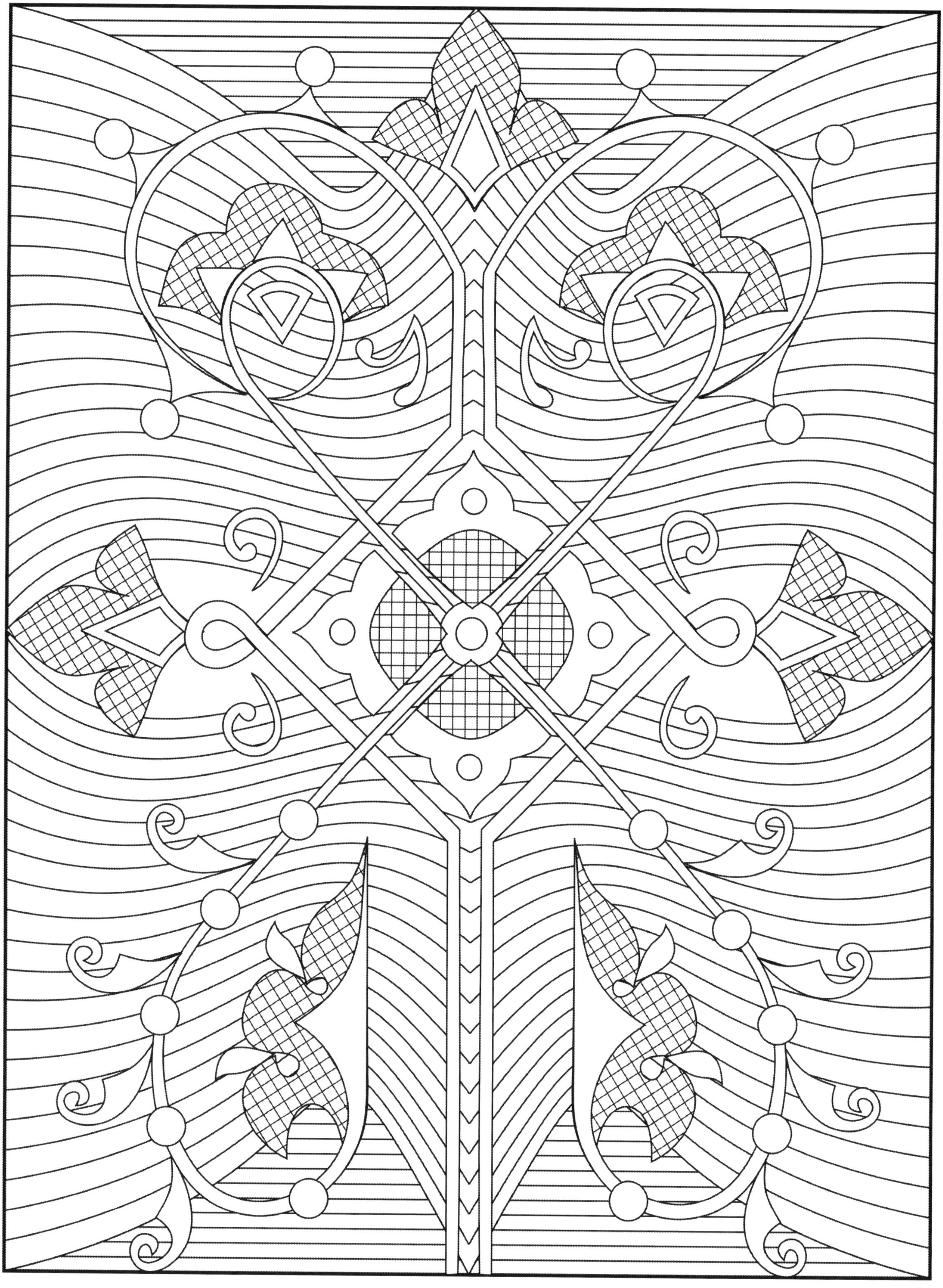

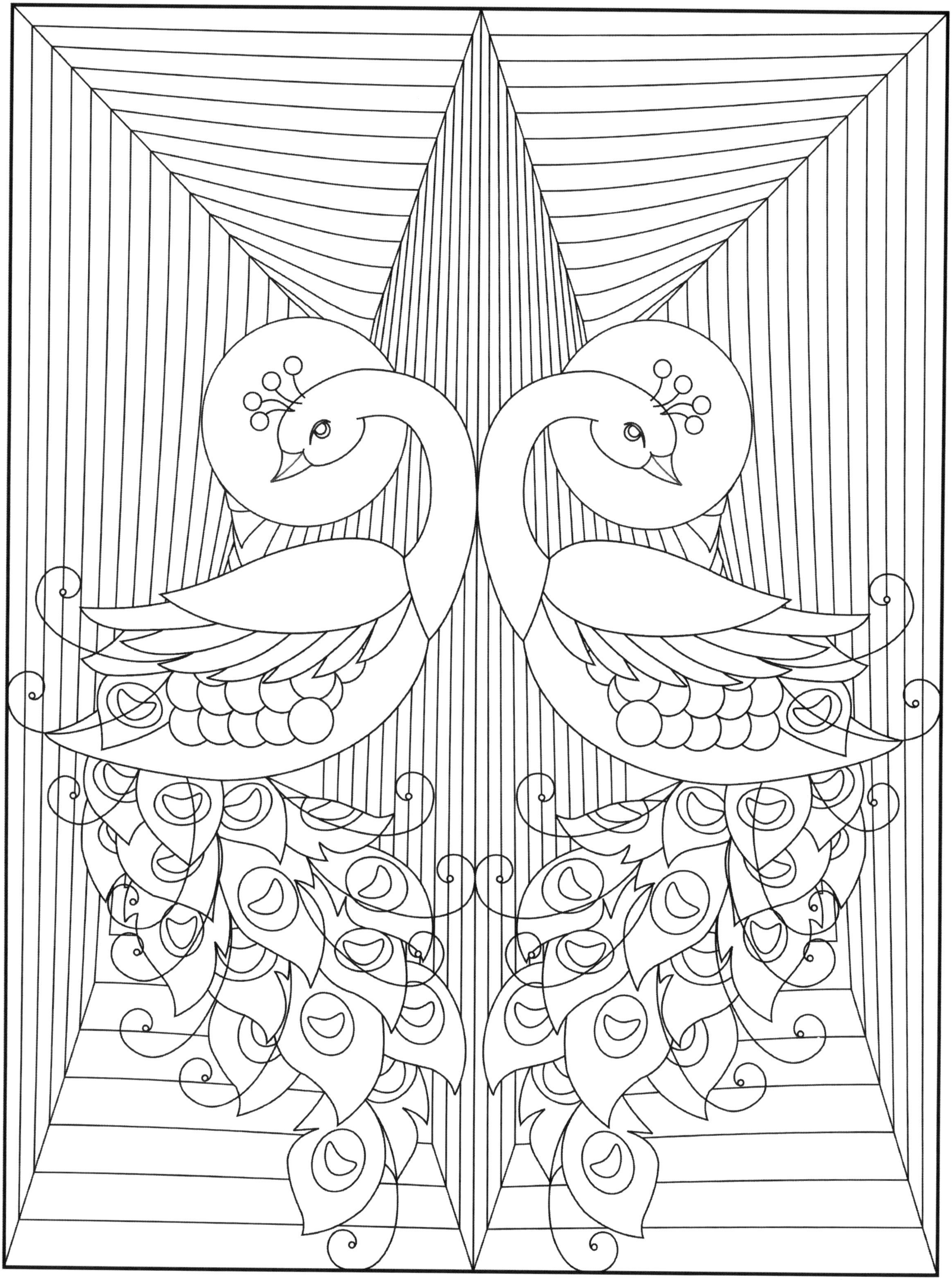

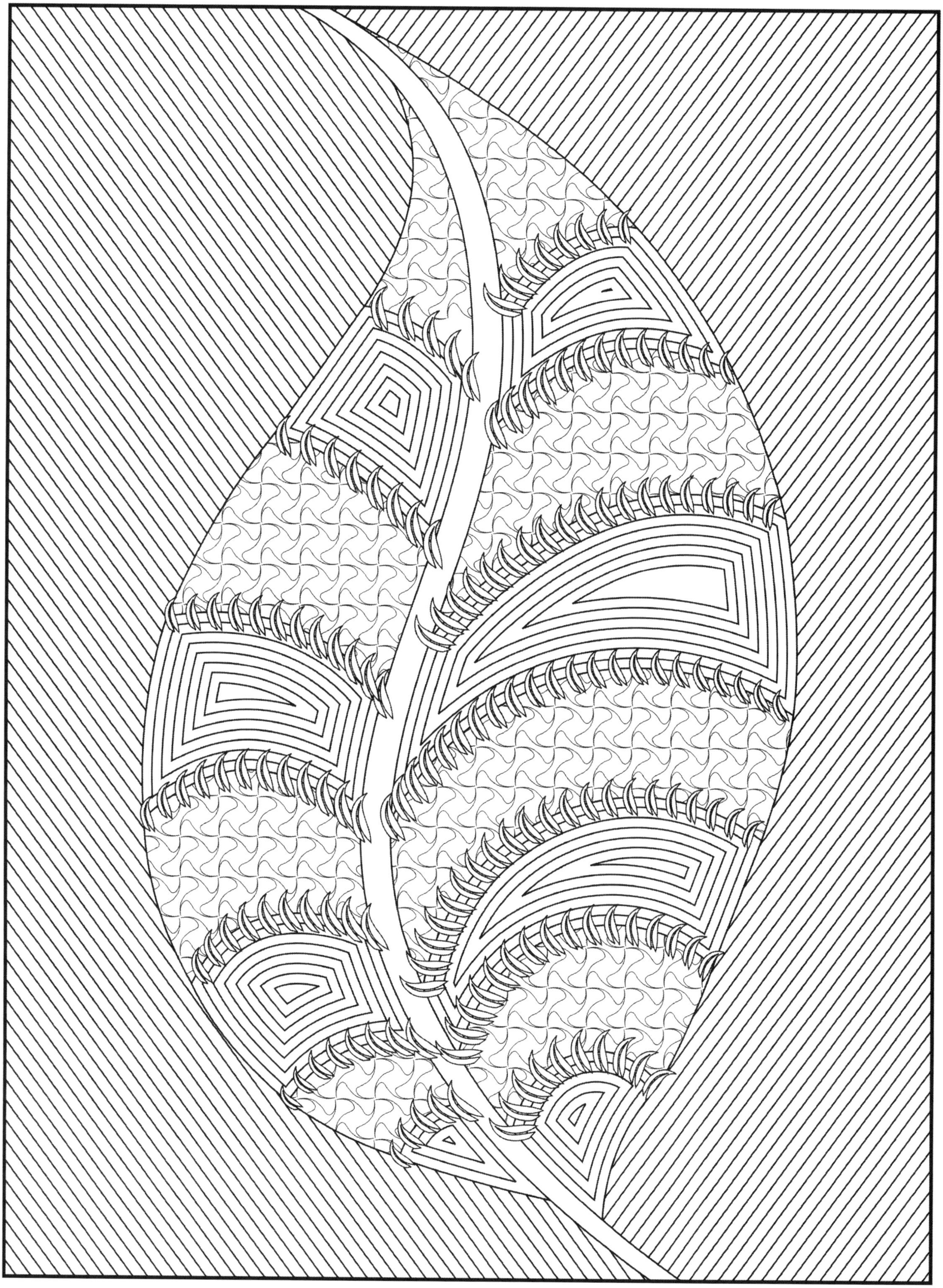

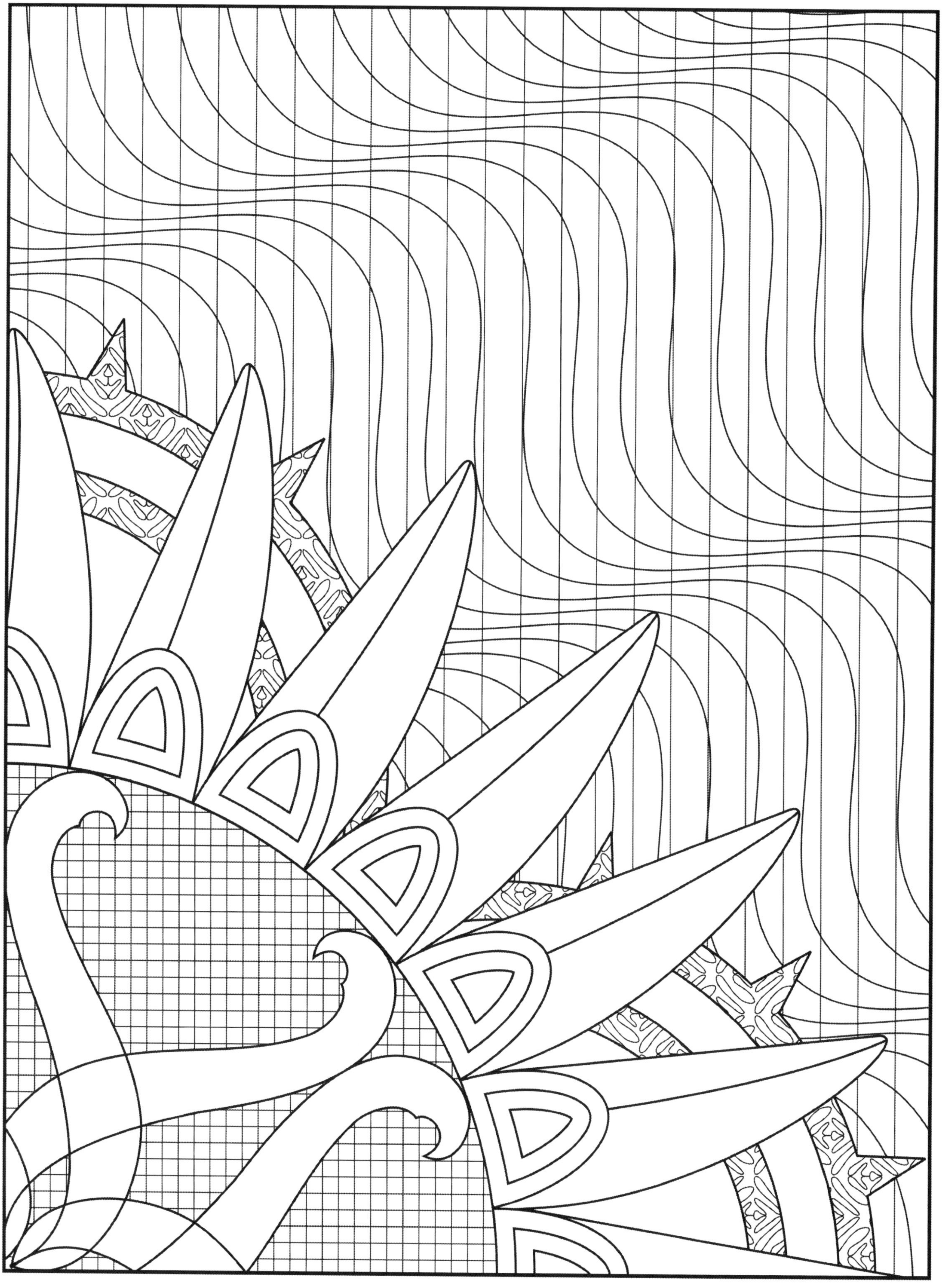

COLOURING TIPS

1. Find a quiet place to do your colouring.
2. Choose your colours according to your liking. Be light and open-minded.
3. Choose to colour in bright natural light whenever possible.
4. Make sure you are sitting in a comfortable seat with good back support. Relax.
5. Don't be afraid to express your creativity. Stress relief colouring is all about fun.
6. Pick your favourite pattern to colour.
7. Colour at a time when you are less likely to be interrupted.
8. If you like classical music, switch it on and play it softly in the background.
9. Choose colouring pencils over regular crayons to do your colouring
10. If you like to use art markers, it is best to use a sheet of craft plastic under the colouring page.
11. Stop colouring whenever you feel like stopping.
12. Whatever the outcomes, it is your masterpiece. Cut it out and frame it if you so desire.

NOTE:

In order to prevent colour-bleeding no images were placed on the opposite side of each artwork.

THANK YOU!

Printed in Great Britain
by Amazon